Replacement Behaviors

Toy Taylor

By Toy Taylor
Printed in the U.S.A

Printed ISBN: 978-1-7330606-5-3

EBOOK ISBN: 978-1-7330606-6-0

Published by: Toy Taylor

Publication: May 2019

Replacement Behaviors

If you are not careful, people will like you and not your behavior.

Introduction

As a child I was labeled as "bad" at a very young age. I had frequent disciplinary infractions at school. I do not remember being rewarded or celebrated for doing anything positive at home. I was always in some way, shape, form, or fashion in trouble.

It was never for one thing either. I used to wonder did people get a kick out of catching me. It was like "the world was against me" type of feeling. What felt worst, I had the intentions to do the right thing. After my offenses, I would mentally agree with myself to do the right thing.

I would still end up right back in trouble despite the mental agreement. It was frustrating. It made for a life of many setbacks and missed opportunities. I wanted to do the right thing internally. The goodness rarely manifested itself externally.
To be completely honest I felt like I had no control. As an adult, I realize I did not. My past frustrations have turned to disappointments. Not in myself though.

When I grew up and left my environment, I was exposed to new worlds. I interacted with new people. People who responded differently to stimuli than people I was previously familiar with. Their behavior was foreign to me. My behavior was foreign to them.

I realized something amazing. My behavior was, and still is at times, highly offensive. Seeing new responses revealed the destructive tendencies of my old responses. It was like a crawling baby seeing a walking baby. I was motivated to walk.
This is where the disappointment set in. Yes, I am in control of my own actions. Even as a child. The issue is my exposure to actions.

I always wanted to be good, but what was good? I wanted to control my temper, but I have two parents that never did or do. I wanted to control my body, but my parents throw beer bottles at each other when they were angry. No lie.

I would have loved to use kind words with my teacher. It was just hard because my parents yelled and cursed each other routinely. I wanted to have a happier demeanor. I just had not seen one during my developmental stages.

I had two parents addicted to drugs and alcohol. The only time they were happy was pay day. They were mean and surly the rest of the days. Especially to us.

We were a part of the problem. We happen to be their children, that had needs. These needs required financial resources. We were chastised for asking for financial resources. Mostly because they had not counted up the cost of having a child. Or been responsible about having sex.

So, I was mostly disappointed with them. I did not know how to appropriately express my anger. I wanted to. Just had never seen it done. Until I left my environment.

My story is common. People are having babies all the time not counting the cost. They are not taking in the consideration for life dysfunctions they are creating. This is the birth place of generational cycles of destruction. Some people call this a generational curse.

Let me say, every single mother is not a bad mother. You cannot control a man. You cannot control life. You have to do what you have to do. A woman cannot predict her husband will cheat and leave her with kids. A wife cannot predict her husband will get sick. Some punches you have to just roll with. It is what it is.

My issue is the voluntary singles mothers. Yes, some woman voluntarily sign-up to be single mothers. Let's look at an example. Though I have many.

Let's say a guy and a girl are dating. While dating, they never lived together. He had multiple girlfriends that she was aware of. Then boom she becomes pregnant.
I am not saying should get an abortion. She should have picked a better boyfriend or chose singleness. When the child comes, his same habits continue, and her life is changed forever. He did not go home to her consistently before the baby, so he does not after. This is why I say there are voluntary single mothers.

They literally sign their kids up for lying, cheating, absent men. The saddest part is their baby feels their bitterness, sadness, and stress. They even argue with the men about habits they were aware of before they conceived. It's never ending for some families.

Is this my reality? No. It was though. I was the child that felt the bitterness, stress, anger, and sadness. When those feelings overbearing in a child's developmental years, it affects them negatively.

I am not psychologist. I am educated. I just have a perspective on this matter because I lived the life. There was no need to study it or become degreed in it.

I will use some scholarly references throughout the selection. However, a majority of my knowledge is lived lessons learned. I realize there are others that want a better life. They even intend to.

The reality is, they find themselves stagnant. Some people are always going "to do" but are never quite achieving anything. Many people have great intentions, but they fall victim to procrastination. Just like when I wanted to be good, but I did not know what good looked like.

Do you think a crack head enjoys being a crackhead? Do you think the heroin addict wants to leave her kid? Someone not on these drugs may think, "how could they do that?" I call it a strong cycle of destructive behavior. Not to excuse it. To lend understanding in hopes of freeing people

There is a process or methodology to breaking cycles of behavior. It is the act of replacing behaviors. Many of us struggle with this from various perspectives.

The mightiest of men have a behavior or two they need to replace. I believe some people want to be better. The just do not have the tools to replace their unprofitable behaviors. For people, self-discipline in one area is no indication there is not addiction in another area.

No one is perfect. We can continuously work to be better. Not better than others, but better than our old selves. This type of attitude can bring the most impoverished generations into sustained wealth.

Notice I said "can". Poverty is real. Replacing destructive behaviors is not easy. If it were, jails would be empty. Sadly, they are filled to capacity. The need for new ones is real.

These men and women do not all come from broken families and homes. Some are very privileged. So, replacing behaviors is not just for those in poverty. The message is bigger than getting rich or making money.

There is a very financially comfortable mom with a temper. There is a wealthy dad that does not know how to be a dad. Replacing behaviors is about continuous growth regardless of your financial status. It is a practice.

Conquering one behavior is only the start. As you progress in life, you will need to filter and sift your behaviors. This is because life changes. When life changes, we have to adjust. Failing to adjust could mean falling behind.

Chapter 1: What is Your Behavior?

To replace our undesired behaviors, we first need to get a good idea of what behavior is. The Merriam-Webster defines behavior as the way in which someone conducts oneself or behaves. I believe this a fine and simple definition. I believe to the general public it is over simplistic.

When you look at the mountains of research that is done on behavior, it is clear there is more to behavior than one sentence can define. I manage a behavior unit on a campus. So, I have been exposed to this mountain of research. It is required for my field. Most people are not.

Their definition of behavior stops at the end of the simple sentence. Rightly so, it is the information they have been presented. There has been no past reason to expand on it. Or at least that is what the unexposed person thinks.

If every man was aware of the power of behavior, it would be at the forefront of their attention. I perceive behavior as the accumulations of images and responses a person is exposed to. I contend that a person's behavior dictates their level of elevation in life. However, those levels are dictated by and limited to said images and responses.

A great example is how I grew up. We had to survive as children. When I say we, I mean my friends and I. Our parents choose between lights and water bills. One would be shut off; it was just a matter of which one they deemed more of a priority at the time.

Most of the time it was the lights. People could not see your lights were turned off from the outside. They could smell you if you could not bath or wash your cloths. Under these conditions, there was not much room for asking our parents for excess good.

Most of the time financial resources were being stretched or nonexistent. So, we did what we "thought" we had to do. In our environment, the older girls had the trendiest clothes because they stole them. So, when we became of age and had the freedom, we stole too.

We had not seen or heard of anyone starting a business. The lemonade stand was a gimmick for suburban girls. Sitting outside with product and money in the hood is like a sitting duck for the hunter. We got what we wanted the same way we saw the people around us; we took.

As I interacted with others that made compensation in a respectable manner, I began to replace my thieving behavior for hard work. This interaction is deeper than just seeing. We all saw people doing better. Yet, I still have friends that shoplift and scheme for a living.

I was forced to interact in a clinical way. I hated then, but I am grateful today. I had a unique experience not afforded to most kids in the hood. My life ended being the polar opposite of my address. Even as I resided there.

I spent the developmental years of my life interacting with loved ones that were trapped in their own destructive cycles and rhythms. Their inappropriate responses and reactions were embedded in me environmentally and biologically. Naturally I emulated what I was familiar with. I was blessed to have people in my life strong enough to absorb my shocks and still teach me appropriate responses.

I was a hot head. Yet, someone not kin to me still had the heart to teach me replacement behaviors. I also had the desire to learn them. I spent my adolescent years learning new behaviors on accident. This teaching came through extraction.

In my book Builder's Code, I explain how the privileged classes afford their children extracurricular activities. These activities are an investment that gives their children an advantage in sports and academics. I know this because these same parents paid for me to participate as well. This was one way I was extracted.

Despite living in the hood, year around I slept in the finest hotels and ate the finest foods. I would have a 6 oz. steak for $100 on Sunday. I was dropped off and eating pork and beans by Monday. Nothing against pork and beans, I'm sure my granny will have some later.

I also had a coach that took a lot of time with me. She treated me as her own. During holidays and summers, I spent days to weeks with her family. I even lived with them for a period of time after college.

Despite growing up in a single parent home, I was extracted and interacted with a married family as a normal. I was able to see how a married couple conducts themselves. I was versed in the position of a wife. I watched and learned the position of a husband.

When I went off to college, I had rich friends who loved me. They had parents that really loved them. I was only used to being yelled at for asking for money. My friends were given allowances worth more than my mom's rent. That showed me the opposite of what I was used to, and that it was possible to have more than I was accustomed to.

My friends were not so lucky to have these imperative interactions. This makes it hard for my friend who has never seen a successful marriage have one. The truth of poor interactions keeps good friends from being good fathers, because they have no idea what that looks like. When you add the cost of survival to that tab, they do not have time to search for those things either.

They cling to the behaviors that have passed the test of their personal times. Change sounds good to the person not paying for the change. So, I understand their plight. I just cannot support it. I support the replacing of such destructive behaviors.

Remember now, I am who I am. I am from where I am from. There are times that I slip back and indulge in destructive behaviors. Sometimes I react just like I was bred to react.

So, I cannot judge anyone. But I will not stay there to appease anyone either. There are too many benefits to growing and becoming better. I am constantly replacing behaviors to become a better me. This replacing, again, is a process.

I am stumped by one thing though. Even if one is in dire environments, like the hood, they can see the end result of that lifestyle. The news, social media, and gossip circles expose it religiously. I wish people would run from that; I did.

I know people that have more talent and skill than me. These people live in situations less desirable than mine because of their behaviors. They fail to replace behaviors that are offensive to their goals. They are loyal to a habit that eroded them slowly.

Behaviors are a double-edged sword. If the right behaviors are applied for the right amount of time, prosperity becomes an inevitable product. Prosperity is not always money. Some people want a prosperous marriage. Others want a prosperous relationship with their kids.

As long as mutual behaviors stay focused on these things, they are possible. Sometimes we fall off track and it is necessary to recalibrate; or replace behaviors. As people grow and change, if they can use replacement behaviors when necessary, the sky is the limit. The failure to do so is quite the opposite.

Failing to replace behaviors can lead to a few unpleasant things. One of them is stagnancy.

All behaviors are not the worst. Some can be distracting from goals, however.

There are people in this world that will "do them" regardless. It is a population of rebels that feel the world should replace its behaviors to adjust to them, not the other way around. I work with these people at work. I interact with them socially. I even love people like this.

This type of person is my motivation to keep replacing my undesired behaviors. When I see the damage of erosion their stubbornness causes, it is frightening. It is almost as if they are blind to their self-destruction. That is not the scariest part.

The scariest part is watching the people they love fail to correct them. Their own parents will see their life is headed in a bad direction because of their poor behavior. They will sit on the sideline and pay for them to continuously indulge in unprofitable behaviors. This is what makes me hard on myself.

When I started to look into the factors of what causes undesirable behaviors, too many of them were voluntary. For example, the suburban parent that pays for the disrespectful child to have fun. That child has no incentive to replace their undesired behaviors, there is no understanding of repercussion.

Replacing behaviors is about choosing and then doing. It is about choosing a better life. It is about committing to one's own excellence. People on the opposite end of this spectrum are complaining about a raise their boss failed to grant them.

Replacing behaviors is more than changing a response or two. It may be changing the environment. It could look like changing associations. It all depends on the type of change that has to be made.

Replacing behaviors is also just a start. After one has mastered replacing behaviors, there is opportunity for new behaviors. New behaviors, if managed properly, can bring new fortunes.

All of this sounds so wonderful. The reality is it takes time, sacrifice, and diligence. If it were easy all men could do it. It takes a resilient man or woman.

Before new behaviors can manifest though, there is still the daunting task of replacing behaviors. This will call anyone looking to replace their behaviors to be overly honest with themselves. They have to be honest about a few things too. A self-evaluation will be necessary.

Some behaviors that need to be replaced are obvious. Like my drinking. There is nothing profitable about me taking shots of tequila. But I like to.

I could realistically replace that budget destroying habit with trading stocks. If I would replace the behavior, my return is double fold. Not only will I earn a profit, I will also learn a new skill. When you apply this type of honesty to a person's life, the sky is the limit.

Will I stop taking shots? No. I like it. It is not at the top of my replacement behavior list at the moment. But I should to support being the best me I can be.

Other undesirable behaviors can be more eluding. An honest self-evaluation of personal behaviors will help a person spot these. After they are spotted, the person has a fair chance to make an informed decision. Like taking shots of tequila.

The self-evaluation is a tool that will help a person identify their destructive behaviors. To each his own. I want to help those that want to help themselves. But they have to help themselves first.

Chapter 2: Profit or Loss? A Look at Your Behaviors

I want to make the reader aware of hypnotic
rhythm as they evaluate their behaviors. I came across this concept while listening to a Napoleon Hill book. Hill described the concept as how habit forms and subconsciously sustain themselves. It suggested that after doing something for so long, it became a part of an individual's hypnotic rhythm.

Like other things in life, hypnotic rhythms can be used for our good or our destruction. The book led me to believe I could control what becomes a part of my hypnotic rhythm. It supports how I feel people can replace their behavior and change their lives. That change is affordable to anyone willing to pay the price. The price is normally whatever it takes.

Do you have what it takes? You want to be wealthy, but do you have the habits of a wealthy person? Do you know what the habits of a wealthy person are? Do you know you can internet search the answer to these questions?

If you have not looked into these very simple things, I would bet you do not really want to be wealthy. It just feels good to think about it. The effort and action required is never really fully applied. This is what separates the successful from the mediocre.

Too many people want a good life. Too few people are willing to even research how to get there. Even fewer get to the stage of self-evaluation and behavior replacement. You reading this is a good sign you want better for yourself.

Self-evaluation and honesty are the best policy. This requires identification of positive behaviors you have. Good can always be better. List attributes you consider a positive part of you.

Make sure they are not all cosmetic. Make sure they are not shallow statements like "Am I a good person?" Have clear and character defining statements like "How am I an asset or support to others?"

Look for places of improvement even with good attributes. Be realistic about improvement. Do not challenge yourself to run five miles a day if you have not run ten meters in four years. Use increments to build up and progress as you go. So, maybe jog a mile, and build up to running five.

There will be some in between behaviors lingering. They will not necessarily be categorized as good or bad. However, if you are completely honest with yourself, or a goal requires optimum focus, a person can categorize them easy.

They can do a profit and loss statement to determine a behavior's worth or validity. A profit and loss statement is clear. What is bringing profit (Good)? What is causing a waste of resources (Bad)? When you add that level of honesty to your behavior, it is a sign of maturity.

The most successful people I know maximize their time. They try to eliminate time wasted daily. These workaholics are still taking work calls during family vacations. Their goals are usually too comprehensive for a small-minded person.

Identifying the negative behaviors may be the hardest. It requires the most honesty. Many of us "like" the behavior, unprofitable or not, that is why we indulge in it.

In a previous book I wrote called The Deceit of Distraction, I gave an example of how an unprofitable behavior had bound me. When I began teaching, I would fuss at my students for playing video games instead of doing their homework. A few years later, I failed graduate school playing the exact same game. Playing that game was what caused me a loss on the profit loss evaluation. I knowingly played it anyway.

Once I had my fill of the game, I returned to graduate school. I replaced my childish behavior with more mature ones like studying. The replacement of behavior in turn awarded me a degree. Had I not replaced my behavior, there would have been no degree awarded.

The negative behaviors go way beyond playing a video game. Like a cheating man. It's like, come on man. If he would do a profit loss inventory, it would show him one bottom feeding woman is not worth his family losses. Yet, I see it all the time.

I meet people bound by addictions. I am friends with women who cheat on their husbands. I know women that leave their children for men who promise no hope of a future. Some people, you do not need a fortune teller or prophet to reveal their future.

Their behavior is a big indication of their impending end. I guess that is the hypnotic part of the rhythm. They probably tell themselves "one day" they will change. Just like I tell myself "one day" I am going to start a diet.

I propose that anyone in the identification stage, do so sober minded and with a sober heart. When we are emotional, we tend to lean towards the self-justification route. This is tricky. We need to make sure we have calm spirits so that we can check the not so calm ones.

After identification, analyze the origin. In simpler terms, figure out where that behavior came from. What is your earliest memory of it? What triggers it? Who did you see act out this particular response?

Now as a disclaimer, I am not a medical doctor. These are suggestions that help me replace behaviors. Some people have deep seeded behaviors that require professional help. Some propensities required trained professionals to intervene.

Be big enough to know when you need help. Seek it when necessary. I have seen therapy do wonders for people very close to me. I also have licensed professionals to speak with. I do not do it alone.

Understanding the origins of the behaviors you seek to replace is a step that cannot be skipped. You need to mentally deal with the circumstance that embedded that response. During this stage you can formulate the appropriate response. Then put it into practice. You can also identify stealthy triggers and work through them.

Next, review the damage that the behavior has caused so far. Has the response broken any relationships? Is the behavior hindering your professional growth? Are you seeing the behaviors in your children?

How do you plan to address these infections? When do you plan to intervene where the undesired behavior has caused disruptions? You might have to go back and make apologies. This is a part of healing.

Do not let your pride stop you here. If you fail to acknowledge your behavior with others, it signals you support your behavior. This is dangerous. Repair as many relationships as you can.

Now, predict future damage that the behavior you need to replace has caused. Think about your goals. Does the behavior help or hurt them? Is it worth keeping the behavior?

What are you willing to give up to get rid of it? Who are you willing to stop seeing so often to let the behavior go? It is not ok to just say you will stop, but stay around people and places partaking in the behavior. That is like a recovering crackhead going to live in a crack house. The temptation is too real.

You have to strategically create a intervention to replace the behavior. Deciding to get over it only, will lead to failure and relapse. Do your best to replace those places and time with those people partaking in undesired behaviors. This is part of "making room" which I will discuss later.

It is best to take it a step further than a intervention plan. Create a time line of completion. It is also better to create a daily schedule. Beating a negative hypnotic rhythm takes more than a thought.

Some behaviors are so embedded people partake in them subconsciously. A smoker can say they will stop smoking tomorrow. If they wake up without a plan, they probably end up taking a smoke break out of habit. They answer the call of their hypnotic rhythm.

Distributors that promise products to break the habit of smoking make billions of dollars for this reason. If it were easy, all smokers would be able to do it alone. People will pay to break hypnotic rhythms. To each his own.

If you can successfully complete the first steps, you might be on a path to replacing undesired behaviors. You may have to rinse and repeat some of the steps as you progress. One unannounced trigger could reset you to your old self. These steps need to be practiced when necessary. This is ok.

The goal is continual progression. Replacing behaviors is like starting and business, it takes time. Most people are so caught up with the get rich gimmick, they fail to put in the time to start a business. Many people are also so "set in their ways" they fail to appropriately replace behaviors.

I challenged myself to better. Even when I slip, I pray and remind myself of my replacement behaviors. It is like a continual resetting process. A funny thing is happening as I get older. The replacement behaviors are starting to become natural and habit.

Gradually I am becoming a better person. I challenge you to too! You only have your life to build. Do not be plagued by old behaviors from old environments.

There is a verse in the Bible that speaks against putting new wine in old wine skins. I attribute this to most things in life. A person has to let go of their old behaviors to step into their new destinations. They risk stagnancy if they do not.

Those old behaviors are not our fault. Well some of them are. That is still no excuse to carry them along in life with us. When you have a good grip on those old behaviors reset yourself!

The world has no interest in "our background" once we offend it. They will accept an apology. They will even be cordial. Still, the scars of our behavior haunt them. Sometimes to a point it holds us back in the future.

This is why I suggest predicting the future damage of old behaviors. It will give one more motivation to reset those destructive rhythms. Replacing behaviors is a tough job. A person needs all the motivation they can get.

This process will feel weird. It is supposed to. You will have to talk to and encourage yourself at times. You might even quit. This is ok, as long as you restart. You only have a better life for you and your generations to gain.

Chapter 3: Threats to Replacing Behaviors

Our behaviors and rhythms are not easily broken all the time. Again, this is why addiction exists. When one has identified their unprofitable rhythms and behaviors, it is now important to replace those old rhythms. The more you know about the rhythm, the easier it might be to break it.

In the previous chapter, I challenged you to identify old behaviors and rhythms. You need to know what you are going to change. I also recommended you review why you need to change it. We identified past damages and future threats the behaviors posed.

I now want to take a look at the nature of the behavior or rhythm itself. The first analysis was personal. This one will be informative. You need information to subdue the rhythm that has for so long, subdued you.

As you make an effort to break rhythms, you will be faced with external difficulties. These externals will be people, places, and things. External difficulties are frustrating, especially when you are already dealing with personal difficulties. External difficulties help breed the personal behaviors and rhythms I brought up earlier. If you sift through the motives of these external circumstances and people, you will save yourself some time.

I want you to think of rhythm in as a musical concept. You can ask someone their favorite song, they can either sing it or hum the melody. That song and its rhythm is embedded in that person's memory. When they hear the song, it triggers memories and feeling. These feeling and memories can be good or bad.

Every individual had a different reaction to their favorite song. Some will break out in a dance routine they made up or mimicked from the artist. Another person might sit down and reminisce on a old friend or beau. Some songs remind me of times my heart was broke. They make me cry.

These rhythms provoke internal feelings that we express externally. As I grow and learn, some songs have less effect from my past. This is because new songs and memories are constantly replacing the old ones. Some people and times I would rather not remember.

49

I actively practice not harping on negative thoughts. Even when I hear a song that reminds me of a bad time, I remind myself of the shut off during the song. I found this to be the best practice. When riding with others or in public, I cannot control what people play. I can control what I think about.

Just as it is with rhythms in music, so it is with rhythms in life. There are places and people that trigger old rhythms and behaviors for you. These triggers give you a feeling. These feelings can be good or bad.

Here is where rhythm differs between music and life. Just like music, these triggers provoke a feeling. That feeling leads to a reaction. However, in life, the reactions are much more dire during bad triggers.

In my behavior unit my students have negative rhythms. Their triggers can be another person getting attention or not getting their way. Their reactions range from lying on the floor crying to throwing heavy school furniture. I have to understand their rhythms to help them.

I help them do what I discussed in the previous chapter. We discuss their antecedents. I help them understand why their reaction was inappropriate. We debrief about the damage. I then teach them replacement behaviors to reset their rhythm.

For years I have noticed that my work has a positive effect. However, those external difficulties have caused many to relapse and return to negative rhythms. It is like no matter how much time I spend with them, once those external difficulties grasp them, the work is undone.

For my students, the external difficulties take on various forms. I have taught 2-year old's to 18-year old's, I noticed a pattern of external difficulties regardless of their age. Some of my best friends are in their 60's. They are plagued by the same difficulties.

The worst external difficulties I see is the ones that people enjoy. Do not be fooled by the word difficulty. That word only speaks to the potential damage it causes. Some people are in love with their difficulties.

Think about a heroin addict. There is nothing good about heroin for anyone but the dealer profiting. The addict themselves are slowly corroding. They risk death with every hit. They are also financially taking a progressive plunge.

These people also have families. Some of them have whole spouses and children. They will leave it all for heroin. They will even steal from their loved ones.

I would call this an external difficulty. The addict is so in love with the drug, nothing else matters. They are caught in the sad rhythm of getting a deathly hit. Often times, the drug use stems from failure to reset the personal rhythms we discussed.

Other people are caught in old rhythms because of the access to resources. I see this mostly in the children. They have no control of their resources. They are dependent upon others for their needs.

A good example I can use is clothing and shoes. When a student does not have the most expensive and up to date styles, they are subject to ridicule. This lack is not their fault. It is just indicative of their parent's financial choices.

Their reaction to this ridicule can range from depression to violence. The personal rhythm that needs to be replaced is the negative feelings about not having what others have. The external difficulty is the parent's lack of resources due to poor choices.

The child would love to change their behaviors like magic. Many difficult children want to do what is right. The truth is they are living in their trigger. The work we do at school is no match for the time spent living with external difficulties. Persistence is key in this case.

I find that some stay bond to negative rhythms and behavior because of their perceived ability. I meet many people that are highly skilled or intelligent. They just fail to see it in themselves. They lead a mediocre life someone probably steered them too.

Everyone is not aware of the unlimited creativity locked inside of us. A big percentage of the population finds one thing that they like and/or are willing to do and stick with it. This is known as a career. I have watched people I love do the same job for 30 years.

This by all means is commendable. Why not go for more though? Why not continuously rise above your own accomplishments? A person has to have perceived value to fight back this difficulty.

They have to dare to want more. They have to be willing to do the work that comes with it. Which leads to my next external difficulty. Too many people are stuck in the rhythm of procrastination.

The Merriam-Webster dictionary defines procrastination as, "to put off intentionally and habitually". Procrastination is such a broad topic I want to focus in on the behavior specifically while replacing behaviors.

Replacing behaviors sounds good. They are good in the long wrong. But procrastination dangles a carrot in front of that "long run". It will steer you to do not necessarily bad things. The task and engagements will be time consuming. This time is vital to accomplishing your dreams in a timely manner, if procrastination takes a hold of you, precious time will slip by.

I call procrastination an externally difficulty because of the many forms it can take. It can look like friends always inviting you out instead of working. It can be pushing back a due date for a client. If you constantly find yourself pushing back what can push you forward, you might be procrastinating about replacing behaviors.

I find that many, young or old, are stuck in rhythms due to their fear of ostracism. I dislike this external difficulty the most. They are so wrapped up in public opinion that they cannot unlock their true selves. People participate in dangerous behaviors to "fit in".

Have you ever heard of a suicide pact? I think it is the most preposterous form of commitment I have ever seen. Yet, it happens. Friends and lovers will make a permanent decision for temporary loyalty. This is an extreme case.

A lighter one is our society in general. Maybe that is not so light. Look at consumer debt. It is all for what? Mostly to buy items to appear to be more than one really is.

A person could take that same debt and purchase investments. However, the allure of "having" or being one that haves, takes precedent. I have lived with people that allowed the lights to be shut off to purchase designer jackets. Just to wear to an event. The struggle was not real, it was voluntary.

I meet some that flat out fear failure. They have access to resources. They have the intelligence and exposure to move forward. They do not necessarily struggle with the rhythms of procrastination and ostracism.

They fear failure. They are happy with life as it is. They see no need to shake things up. They fear the external difficulties they cannot control.

You can spot these people easy. They are highly successful in the profitable behaviors they do partake in. They are also staunchly bound to their not so profitable behaviors. They have little to no interest in replacing behaviors or resetting rhythms.

I suspect that one day I will feel this way about some things. Currently, I am on a quest to becoming better. This requires me to be honest about all unprofitable behaviors and rhythms that hold me back. I have to weather through the external difficulties mentioned above like anyone else.

I understand if I do not work diligently to replace unprofitable behaviors, I am ultimately taking a loss somewhere, even if I add profitable ones. The unprofitable behaviors either steal from or infect the profitable ones. Negative rhythms have to be reset with diligence. I recognize I stick to most of my negative rhythms because I like them.

I have to constantly remind myself of my goals and future despite what I like. It is a constant battle to do what is right opposed to what you want. I do not want to give you the impression this process is easy. Keeping a measurable and attainable goal helps the process.

When I try to replace a behavior without a goal or incentive, I tend to be laxed about the behavior. So are others. You may have to motivate yourself to replace behaviors that you know are not conducive for you. This is ok.

You do whatever it takes to break unprofitable rhythms.

A goal is not the replacement behavior itself. It is the expected end for utilizing the replacement behaviors. Goals are our treasure and our behaviors are the treasure map. The two have to interact to navigate through personal behaviors and external difficulties.

Chapter 4: Failure & Goals while Replacing Behaviors

I have the degrees to prove that I am a researcher. Instead of giving you paragraphs filled with statistics I will speak solely from experience. I grew up around numerous people I consider failures. I can even pinpoint why they failed.

It would be awesome if I could just reveal the truth to them. The reality is, they are not looking for the truth. If they were, they would not be continuously partaking in the behaviors that lead to their failures. So, I will just reveal the truth to you.

Mind you, I am not equating success to money. By that definition I am a failure as well. I just know people that struggle that were smarter and more talented than me. It breaks my heart in the humbled way.

Many of them have no goals or direction. Even when presented with opportunities, they stick to behaviors that are familiar. These familiar behaviors are often counter-productive to the opportunities. They do this despite knowing the assets the opportunities bring.

All failure is not bad failure. Some failures teach priceless lessons to ready learners. I am specifically talking about the people that fail to replace behaviors. They forfeit profitable goals for old behaviors and rhythms. I have done this myself before.

In my opinion time is the biggest factor. Setting goals and replacing behavior takes time. Many times, people opt for negative behaviors to achieve goals. This is an attempt to cut time or perceived parts of the process.

There is enough history available to caution these types of behavior. Yet, the news exposes every day that people still partake in them. These behaviors are often labeled as crime. Everyday some individual believes they are lucky enough to outwit the universe.

Sadly, the universe is deceitful. It will even allow this individual to successfully partake in such behaviors successfully for a bit. I believe this is because that person is just playing a role that the universe needs played in another negative or positive parallel. Then after the universe is done, it calls in that person to collect its debt.

This debt looks like failure. It can sometimes be confused with the failure that comes from attempting profitable goals. It is important to discern between the two. Failure to discern could lead to negative behaviors from personal frustration and spite.

After you understand failure, you stay on track to replacing your behaviors even more. Define your goals as you go. It is ok to change your mind or your course as you need to. At this point you should be aware of the procrastination and ostracism this change will bring.

Defining your goals is a critical step in replacing behaviors. As I mentioned in the previous chapter, you need to know where you are going. Your behavior plays a major part in getting you there. I left goals for after identifying personal and external behaviors on purpose.

Having goals without starting the healing process can be a regressive approach. It is like going into a fight blind. You can have the best intentions, if you are not aware of your own weaknesses, it can cost you. I would rather you pay the cost up front.

My first step in defining my own goals is assessing my wants. I literally ask myself "what do you want?". When I first began the process of replacing my behaviors, my wants were pretty immediate. I wanted things like a better living situation.

I wanted to have more desirable clothing. That called for wanting a better career. This led to wanting an education. As I progressed, I realized my wants did as well.

I noticed that hitting my goals was indicative of the behaviors I partook in as I got older. For example, I have friends that were better athletes than me. We all had a goal to play college sports on scholarship. However, I was one of few in my graduating class to be awarded a scholarship.

We all talked about it because it sounded good. I believe my teammates and classmates actually wanted. We all engaged in different behaviors in terms of teaching that goal. I had one friend who only practiced with our school during season.

There were other teammates that did that and played summer league. I had a few that were even willing to do extra gym work with me on top of that. I just did not have one friend that consistently worked with me. They let external difficulties get in the way of the goal.

I ate, breath, and slept my sport. I left practice of one sport and went to practice my strong sport after. I remember getting in from a track meet at 1 am and leaving for a volleyball tournament at 3 am. Game time was at 8 am. And I played; sleep or no sleep.

I played every chance I had. I played at recreations centers and college dorm sand courts. If I had no access to the gym, I would do weight or cardio training. I had no time to behave like the others. In the end, I got my scholarship.

It is not enough to just have the goals, the behavior has to go with it. Knowing who you want it for also helps replace those behaviors. It is ok if you want it for yourself. I did.

I think what trips people up is, what they are willing to replace. This is why I suggest having goals during the process of replacing behaviors. Maybe monks have the discipline to do the right thing with no return all the time. I see the momentous discipline that has to be applied for nuns to vow to their faithfulness.

I do not have that. I consider myself to be have faith. I still need a little incentive to focus. I feel anyone caught in the throes of addiction or destructive rhythms lack strong desires and goals. Goals help me get out of the bed in the morning.

Even when someone has decided to replace behavior and rhythms, they have one more nagging question. For how long? How long are they willing to wait to achieve that goal? What opportunities, or perceived opportunities, are they willing to miss for their goal?

If the answer is not, "however long it takes", they are in trouble. The goal can be replacing a temper with peace. The goal could be hitting their cat in the face with cheese.

Without the right diligence, all the identifying, analyzing, and planning is a waste.

Those that put in the right amount of time, see the expected reward. As an individual you have to decide your own personal timelines. I must admit, sometimes you will abandon a goal. I think this is fine if it is not leaving a profitable goal for an unprofitable one.

After making certain commitments to yourself, research what it takes to get there. I hope this is not wrong. If I want to be rich, but I am poor, chances are I act like a poor person. I think like a poor person.

There was nothing wrong with this, until I decided I wanted to be rich. I have to purposely research for habits and propensities of rich people. I have to commit to replacing poor behaviors with rich ones to attain my goals to be rich. Doing the same poor things will breed the same poor results.

Do yourself a favor, identify those unprofitable behaviors as early in life as you can. You only have the rest of your life to live. Be honest during this stage. If you are not, it will manifest itself later in the process.

No matter if they are personal behaviors or external difficulties, commit to replacing unprofitable behaviors. Keep your goals in focus. Take as much time in the process as you need to. Just make sure you are taking time to understand and not time to procrastinate.

After that, understand and define your goals. It is essential for the next stage. I touched on replacing behaviors earlier in this chapter when I have the rich and poor scenario. That is just a film over the wealth of information it takes to replace behaviors.

Replacing behaviors sounds good, but replace them with what? You even have to start replacing your what. All these replacements should be in contradiction of the unprofitable behaviors we previously identified. They should disrupt the rhythms that bound us to stagnancy.

This is a critical step. Failure at using a behavior to replace a behavior is detrimental. Most people confuse replacing behaviors with "stopping" a behavior. Replacement behaviors should be in direct alignment with your defined goals.

Chapter 5: Making Room for Replacement Behaviors

Earlier in the book, I suggested you take a few steps. I thought that these steps were necessary before one dives into replacing their behavior. When you replace something, the old thing is no longer there. The replaced thing takes the vacated position.

I wanted readers to replace their unprofitable behaviors. Therefore, I need them to remove the old behaviors first. They needed to be identified as "needing replacement". Then, there would be room for the replacement behaviors to inhabit.

This reminds me of a passage in Matthew 12. The passage explains a how a demon left a man. When it left it found that it had no wear to go. The demon decided to return to the man. The demon found the man was still clean.

Upon the demons return, he brought back some friends. The man did as I advised my readers, he identified the "demon" or not good thing. He had to have identified it. He had deliberately put it out.

He had "made room" or "made clean, depending on the text translation you read. However, he failed to replace the clean area with something new. This passage pronounced my point about replacing behaviors. The demon and its friends would not have been able to renew their lease if the man had occupied the space.

It is the same concept with behavior. It is not enough to just "stop" the unprofitable behavior. One cannot expect to just break a rhythm without replacing the tune. This replacement is critical. If previous steps were skipped, there might not be enough room for the replacement behaviors.

Replacement behaviors have to align or contradict everything we previously discussed. You have to have a good understanding of what your behavior is. If not, you will not know what to look for. Missing critical information about replacing your behavior could cause a setback. You may not understand your slander hurts people until you are sued, if you miss identification of that behavior.

After you have a good understanding of behavior, you can identify your own that are unprofitable. You will be able to sift through and throw out the negative ones efficiently. This is critical to making room for the replacement behaviors.

I suggested defining goals before initiating replacement behaviors as well. I think it would be hard to behave not knowing for what reason. The reason gives the how. The reason is normally a goal.

After the goals are defined, one can set the course toward how they should act and react. The accumulation of these steered actions and reactions in turn deliver the defined goals. The only people that fail are the ones that fail to finish or amend their goals accordingly. This may require more replacement of behaviors as an individual develops.

It is now time to specifically focus on the replacement behaviors themselves. Now that you have room for them. A replacement behavior is more dynamic than cutting down your coffee consumption. It can be that simple. It often entails more.

I will continue to use coffee to expound upon the point. Hypothetically, I drink too much coffee. I have three cups in the morning. I have two cups at lunch. I often have a cup after my dinner, hypothetically.

That is a lot of coffee consumption. For me. That is also a lot of prep throughout the day. This is time that has to be replaced. All of those coffee breaks are without a doubt part of my hypnotic rhythm.

I have to purposely have a replacement behavior for those times. Like maybe drinking tea. Or I could commit that time to working out. It does not sound like much time. I promise it is twenty-five minutes to an thirty if I make my coffee at home. Stopping for coffee adds more time.

That time could be used for a myriad of things. When I began replacing behaviors, my collected time was used for writing. I understand everyone is not a writer. Each individual has to do whatever floats their personal boat.

As a recovering coffee addict, I may have to replace the places I frequent. Instead of

75

meeting at a coffee shop, meet a friend at a bakery. You could even go to a sandwich shop. The local shops are the best.

Meet in places that expose you to other cultures. Go where ever you like really. I just suggest you do not sit in the aromas of a coffee shop. Especially when you are first kicking the habit.

When all of your coworkers are meeting for their routine coffee circle, have your replacement beverage in hand. Anytime I did not have a replacement, I indulged in the undesired behavior. I would kid myself that I would go back to being disciplined the next day or time. You have to be proactive or overly disciplined.

When you start to replace your old behaviors, something funny will happen. It will happen with people. As you change, so will they. Some for the good, and some for the worse. You see people's real intentions or feelings as you make profitable changes.

This leads to a hard one. You may even have to replace people. Even people you love. Now notice I did not say throw them away. We will go more in-depth about this later.

I will stick to the coffee example right now. You may have some strong-minded friends that prefer a coffee shop despite your fight to do what is right. They may give you a "their way or no way" ultimatum. Be sure to take your way if you need to.

You might be strong enough to go and have a chai tea while your friend sips a fresh brew. I am not. If I go to the coffee shop, I want my expresso shot in whatever I order. I always add extra whip cream and caramel. I love coffee.

If you are like me, you might have to find a new chat buddy. There are no hard feelings towards your coffee buddy. That buddy is just not conducive to kicking your coffee addiction. You have to find a jogging buddy perhaps. It depends on what you use to replace the coffee.

Another thing that may need replacement are the events you frequent. I can give so many examples. I will resist the urge to explain going to church after the night club. I will, again, stick to the coffee example.

Since I am a real coffee enthusiast, hypothetically, I attend coffee industry events. I like to taste imported coffee at these events. This helps me make informed coffee purchasing decisions.

It may be best to cancel my imported coffee membership while I work on my habit. Unless coffee is a part of my income. Then, extreme restraint will have to be practiced. You have to pay your bills.

I suggest finding events that align with the individual's goals. They are getting a double return on their time. They are phasing our undesired behaviors. At the same time, they are gaining new knowledge and skills. Knowledge and skills are profitable.

Constantly turning down old invitations can be hard. Use this as an opportunity to create new ones. Invite friends to participate and engage in your new normal. Whatever that might be.

As you interact in your new environments with your replacement behaviors, you will attract like-minded people. This is not to say you will never be approached by an idiot. Distractions are everywhere. We will discuss that next. You are just naturally putting yourself in the lane of like-minded thinkers.

Once you get in the stride of actually replacing the undesired behaviors and rhythms, remain consistent. The route may become boring. Other routes may present themselves as more glamorous. Constantly review your goals.

I mentioned earlier in the selection you might have to change your mind. You might have to reroute your course. I still stand behind that though I am saying stay consistent. I think you should recalibrate when necessary.

I just want you to be careful not to quit. As you start to replace behaviors, the external and personal difficulties will amplify themselves in the beginning. This is natural, you are looking for them so that you can replace them. Just remember to replace the behavior after you are triggered.

You will probably fail the first couple of times you try. Because of this, you also need perseverance. Persevere and carry through when you feel like quitting. Relapsing is easy. You have to fight to keep going.

The more consistent you are, you will feel the results. The more you persevere, you will see the results. You will gradually see your triggers have less effect on you. I want to remind you I am not a license mental health specialist. You may need help outside of the suggestions that helped me.

Eventually, your replacement behaviors will become your new hypnotic rhythm. At least that is the goal. You want to replace the old behaviors with the new ones you deem more profitable to you.

Most of these concepts are supporters of your overall self-discipline. Self-discipline will fortify the replacement behaviors as they become more permanent. The becoming permanent is gradual. Most people want it to be instantaneous.

During your process, you will slip back. You will catch yourself engaging in the behaviors you seek to replace. I believe this is different from a failure. Well, unless you stay back.

Do not be ashamed to keep trying. Let me causation you now. People will see you fail. O well. Dust yourself off a keep trying no matter what. You will have to constantly rise above opinions during this process.

You will also be exposed to new behaviors as you interact in your replacement environments. You will pick up replacement techniques through engaging with replacement people. You can choose to use them or not. Just keep a good balance of behaviors that are profitable for you.

Chapter 6: Distractions while Replacing Behaviors

I wish I could tell you that you replace your behaviors, and everything will be fine. The process is not over. There are distractions that will present themselves as you develop the replacement behaviors. New frequencies will seek to make themselves a part of your new rhythm.

They will present themselves in various forms. The distractions will seep in through multiple areas of your life. Distractions are deceitful in this way. They are stealthy.

Some distractions will be spiritual. These types of distractions try the foundation of your faith. They seek to drag you to a state of unbelief. If this is done successfully, you are open to accept whatever the opposition wants you to believe.

It is not a full-on attack on your faith. It is a gradual wearing down. Most faiths preach against moving away from doctrine for this reason. Some people see it as strict. Others see it as safe.

The ones that deem it safe to stick with doctrine understand the concept of replacement behaviors. They understand to stay closer to faith is to be faithful. They can see dabbling in other movements can lead to losing faith. Some people will say they will replace their doctrine to listen to a song for instance.

I believe this is not evil. I listen to songs that are contradictory to my faith. I am still working on some areas. I am careful not to replace too much of it over my doctrine. I believe I become what I inundate myself with.

When dealing with your spirituality, you have to watch your time. You have to make sure other replacement behaviors are not in contradiction to your faith. You want to be better. Not worse over here to be better over there.

As time progresses, mental distractions will present themselves as well. An individual has worked themselves up to replacing their behavior at this point. They should be aware of these old triggers. As they interact and engage in new environments, they have to beware of new triggers.

The trigger will not announce itself. You will know its presence when you react in an old way in your new environment. You have to pluck that negative weed quickly. Find its root and pluck it.

Mental distractions are those inner thoughts that are negative or unprofitable. They can lead to lost opportunities and mental illness of not managed. I quickly replace positive thoughts for mental distractions when I can. Sometimes I am so upset, the negativity runs rampant for a bit.

It is ok to be sad. It is ok to feel hurt. These are human feelings. They help us regulate our emotions. Even though they are the less desirable emotions.

It is dangerous to not replace these thoughts and emotions with positivity. Negative thoughts feed negative frequencies into your rhythm. You have to continuously put a stop to it. Replace those thoughts with future building thoughts on purpose.

Social distraction is another area of concern. The same social mediums that have the ability to distract us, also have the ability to propel us. I can use social media as an example. Millions of people get on social media daily for entertainment.

Yet, there are millions of people that also use it for commerce daily. If the entertainment seekers would replace their task for commerce, their lives would improve. This is not how the world works though. To each his own.

You have to be careful of social distractions when you are replacing behaviors. Interacting socially is a behavior itself. If the interactions do not equate to profit, they are entertainment. Replace entertainment for profits until your profits pay for your entertainment.

Replacing behaviors can even affect your finances. You may want to purchase your first house. If you have spending habits that take away from your down payment, you have to replace them. They have to be replaced with behaviors that build your down payment budget.

Financial distractions will seek to destroy that down payment budget. They are not seemingly harmful distractions either. A new shirt here and small vacation there add up. When people look at the money they spend over ten years, they could have paid for their homes in cash.

Financial replacement behaviors can help with many endeavors. A person just has to be mindful of financial distractions that will arise. They have to be willing to ride the wave of people's opinions when replacing financial behaviors. When people change their spending habits, others can tell.

You may have to use replacement behaviors in your relationship. We all come from different homes. Many mates come from different backgrounds. Sometimes people cross cultures. This will mean the definition of a relationship will be different between the parties.

If this was not so, there would be no divorce. All relationships would be bliss. Instead, finishing is only reserved for a few. The couples that can successfully utilize replacement behaviors in their relationship may avoid divorce court.

Relationship distractions present themselves in different stages of a relationship. The distraction is not always another person. It can be a new habit the partner is not fond of. If one partner is not able to replace their behavior it could cause friction.

We are sometimes guilty of indulging in voluntary distractions. Notice I said "we". Sometimes I feel justified to "do what I want to do". I will waste a little time to feel good or reward myself.

I think this is ok. I obviously think it is ok because I do it. I understand I have to manage this though. Over indulgence is fatal to my goals.

Some people feel justified for too long. Before they know it, their little indulgence is a big part of their rhythm. For this reason, you have to watch all distractions. I have seen people go too far. It helps me stay balanced.

A distraction is like the cheating man. He convinces himself he will only cheat one time.

After all, his wife will not find out about one time. So he thinks.

Getting away with that one time is intoxicating. Now he is convinced if he keeps the same pattern, along with his normal rhythms, he will be fine. Almost always, the cheating manifest itself. The many "one" times and "last" times add up to years of infidelity.

It comes across to his wife as an era of disregard for her in the marriage. All that is lost is not worth the first time. All who are hurt can barely heal wondering when the next time will be. That is how a distraction can be.

If people could count up the cost while distracted, more people would get to work. Many stumble into latter life wondering where it all went wrong. Some truck along hoping a miracle will save them during retirement years. Both parties should have replaced unprofitable behaviors in their younger years. They pay for it in their latter years.

As you see distractions present themselves, avoid them. Avoid them with replacement behaviors. The sooner they come up the better. The longer you indulge, the more time it has to graft with your rhythm.

You have to be careful that new distractions do not infect current replacement behaviors. When this happens, you risk setbacks and failure. Use the same technique that you use to analyze behavior for distractions.

Chapter 7: Directing Your Replacement Behaviors

From the time you start replacing behaviors, until you finish, every person, place, or thing is a distraction or an opportunity. Let me give my disclaimer. This is not a license to put your nose in the air. It is not cool to treat people as if they have lesser value.

Everyone should be treated the same. And yes, I am not the nicest person sometimes. I am trying to be better every day. I am still working on it with the people I perceive "asked for it".

You do have to guard your time and investments during distractive encounters. You have to possess discernment each interaction. Stay open. What starts out as a distraction could open the door for an opportunity. That is why is say watch how you treat even those you perceive inferior.

If you discern it is purely a distraction that is only taking from you, then yes, cut it off. Serve it from a distance. You may have to do this to people you love. I do not just mean in terms of money.

Some people will pull from your emotions, peace, and integrity. In my opinion they are not worth it. Necessities and expense can be mailed if they need help. That is just my philosophy. To each his own.

If it is an opportunity, then you can relinquish more of yourself. Some opportunities will be as conspicuous as stop signs. Others are not discovered until sufficient time has been spent. But you have a sense the whole time if an opportunity is present.

Take time to evaluate all opportunities. This is another ploy to conserve your time. All opportunities do not hold the same weight. All opportunities require differing amounts of time and resources.

Start by ranking each opportunity as they appear. You should have other opportunities presently flowing. They should be flowing toward your goals. Put opportunities that align closest to your goals closest to the top in rankings.

You can decide its value after you align it. The opportunities value can depend on a few things. Will it get you to your goal faster? Will it support another opportunity? Has the new opportunity caused the old opportunity to become obsolete?

There are many questions you could ask yourself to determine value. Your questions are dependent on your individual goals. Make sure to do your research. Time invested in research is time saved during interaction.

You can use opportunities to position yourself. In my life, opportunities have come from who I know. Some opportunities will be making yourself familiar with people who have access to positions you desire. Be careful of your motives. Form genuine relationships if you take this route.

The cell phone and social media has made being genuine automated at this point. You can send group text during holidays. Social media will alert you of birthdays. Just make room in your schedule for social interaction.

You can now do it from the comfort of your couch.

There will be times that you brush up against failure. You will do everything you know possibly right. Failure will still come knocking. This is not the worst thing. Even though it feels like it.

At some point you will miss something during your evaluation of an opportunity. Some defective things will only present themselves after you have invested. Like a good girlfriend that is a terrible wife. Not to bash women, men disguise themselves too.

This does not mean you are done for. Unless you decide to be done for. I believe some people mistake setbacks for failure. Any sign of unpleasantness sends them in a spiral.

It is only failure if they give up in my opinion. What some people call failure, I deem as a learning experience. Sometimes it is a natural quality control mechanism. Setbacks and perceived failures are like leaks discovered on a ship.

This can be beneficial, especially if the leak is discovered before the ship sets sail. In real life, those leaks need to be fixed. They can slow a person down while reaching their goals. It could also hinder them from reaching them completely.

As in a ship, look for the cause for your "leak". What caused the setback? Was is a personal or external cause? What behaviors need to be replaced? What steps need to be taken to get back on schedule?

You might discern something is a distraction and still dabble in it. You may partake a little here. You might enjoy a little there. You know you. If you lack self-control dabbling is dangerous.

The less self-control you have, the more susceptible you are to relapsing into old behaviors. All the hard work on the replacement behaviors are not lost. They will be harder to get back to the more you dabble. This is why you have to be careful.

Dabbling in distractions is like digging yourself in a whole. If you keep digging with no plan or regard, you will find yourself stuck in it. You can call out for help if someone is near. You just have to hope you have the fee they will require.

In this age, not much is free. Even family members demand gas money if you want a ride. I do not think this is because they are conservative. I think it is the exact opposite.

They want you to replenish the resources they need to deplete on themselves. At times you will be blessed. Strangers do nice things. Some people will give a handout if they have it.

An individual cannot depend on this. If there is no one close to lend a free hand, the ditch digger risks being stuck. Just like people in this world. They give so much time and effort to distractions they have few resources when opportunities present themselves.

I propose a period of recalibration to alleviate pressures of distractions and opportunities. I recommend this for a few reasons. Recalibration is beneficial for time conservation. It is like a periodic review of who you are.

It is a way to keep the consistency in your process I mentioned earlier. Goals should be reviewed during recalibration. Get a since of where you are going before you decide where you are. This is a time to make goal amendments if necessary.

It will not always be an amendment. Sometimes you will make no changes. Some goals you will send to the waste basket. It is all dependent on the individual.

You can turn your sights to where you are after you have refreshed where you are going. Recalibration is a time to align the two. Especially if you have made changes to where you are going. Throw out task that are not essential to your goals. An opportunity can turn into a distraction.

Review your progress with your replacement behaviors as well. Are they working? If not, why? Is more replacement needed? What changes are you willing to make?

Before you close out your calibration, set the next recalibration date. Hold yourself accountable. This is personal progress monitoring. Time is very stealthy. It will pass you by. You will not notice until the accomplishments of others grab your attention.

Because of this truth, it is more profitable to stay focused on opportunities. Distractions are deceitful as well. They give you control until you have no control. Then it is unintended work to get back to your opportunity.

I find that people's level of distraction sometimes depends on their resources. I can use my work with children as an example. The kids that have more, are less driven. They are more worried about keeping up their fashions than their grades.

My students who are less fortunate have a different demeanor. They are less distracted and disruptive. Some because they do not want to draw attention to themselves. Most are on a mission. They are trying to get an education to escape their current conditions.

It seems to me the survivor is concerned with their opportunities. I believe the well-kept tend to gravitate toward distractions. There is always one or two that stand out. They are well kept and driven. This is rare.

Make sure that your replacement behaviors are commissioned for opportunities. The more you focus on your goals, the closer you come to obtaining them. It is that simple. With added effort of course.

Too many talented people that I love are missing out on life. They are stuck in distractions. They let their old behaviors infect new opportunities until they died off. I can be further in life myself. So, my intention is not to judge.

I want to inform and help others. Many people do not know the process to unlocking their fullest potentials. My way may not be the best way. It is just the way I have taken. It is the way that has helped me reach my goals.

Be careful with opportunities that push you to distractions. Some opportunities seem overwhelming and impossible. Some people will settle for a distraction instead. This is a mistake.

Use the concept of small pieces. When you add many small pieces together, they accumulate to one big piece. You have to have this feeling about big goals. You may have to break it down into pieces.

You do what you can while you can. After a while those pieces will come together as the whole goal you envisioned. Do not settle for distractions. Stick with your goals and watch opportunities will appear out of seemingly nowhere.

Chapter 8: Manage People Instead of Replacing People

I wanted to save a whole slot for people. If you follow the same principals for behavior previously mentioned, you will replace everyone. You will never form meaningful relationships that way. Relationships are like keys to your goals.

People are fickle. One moment they could be on top of the world. The next year they could be a beggar. A few bad decisions is the cause of this most of the time.

Life's circumstance can cause some to fall as well. I have a friend who's husband had been diagnosed with cancer. They were both healthy in their forties. They did not see this coming.

The point I want you to grasp is, sometimes people will be up and sometimes they will be down. You have to be careful how you treat a down person. You never know when life will take them up. That is why it is best practice to treat all people equally.

I show the janitor the same respect I show my principal at school. I help them clean the school when I have to too. I understand we are a community. I need them at times. I want them to know we are serving each other.

I am not perfect. I have not treated every single person right. I am not proud of this. I just try to continually get better at it.

Some people make the mistake of only being kind to people there perceive is an asset. They do not take the opportunity to get to know others. They are making a grave mistake. I learned this as I grew and matured.

You never know who knows who. It is not about the person themselves. It is who they may know. You have to be conscious that they may have a connection down the line.

As I grew older, I realized it may be years, but a person might know the right person when you need them. The universe will allow you to stumble upon it too. I have been talking to people with no intentions. Just talking.

During the conversation, I will present a problem. The person will say "You know what,

I know such and such", without me asking. It is a product of building relationships and networking with people. It is also a pure blessing.

The problem with people is, they are people. They do things. They get up under your skin. They tell lies. They are jealous about things they will not work for.

They will do all of the aforementioned things and smile in your face. They will shake your hand and assure you all is good. The whole time they are stabbing you in the back and the head. After that, you are supposed to still be professional.

There will be some spirits and some people you have to extract from your life. Period. You will know who they are. Then there are others.

There are some people who will offend you. However, it is more profitable to repair the relationship than replace them. You will know by their alignment to your goals. It will be possible if the wound they inflicted is not too fatal.

This type of person has obviously shown their true colors. There is no need to paint over them. A fresh coat will not help. You can govern yourself accordingly.

Instead of cutting people off or replacing them, work on cutting them back. Try not to give your trust too freely. Give it at a cost. If it is broken, keep it from that person. You do not have to trust someone to say hello.

Lead on a relationship with the person as if everything is perfect. It is best to politely decline invitations. Do not give them much information about you. Always be nice.

You never know when life will bring you two across each other's path. You never know who will be up and who will be down. Keep it in a space that they can only speak highly of you when the time comes. If they happen to lie, it will reveal itself. The universe is like that.

Replace the unhappy thoughts about this person with other thoughts. You can think about your peace you should be protecting. You could think about a profitable idea or investment. You could even read instead and increase your knowledge.

You have to practice replacement strategies with some people. You have to try to reserve your reputation regardless of the relationship climate. Again, people are fickle. They will project energy at you not intended for you.

It would be nice to cut everyone off and live on a private island. Or at least that is my fantasy. I am an introvert. The reality is I have goals.

My goals need people to come to fruition. I have to work together with others to achieve my goals. There may be people who have achieve momentous success alone. I have not met them. The successful people I know recommend building relationships.

If you have to replace someone, it does not have to be indefinite. Some offenses require temporary replacement rather than cutting back. They will probably be cut back if they are allowed back though. It is a reason you had to temporarily replace them.

This act of mercy is for people who have made a change. Not just a three day "hold it together" change either. I mean a real change.

They need to demonstrate they have successfully replaced undesired behaviors.

Expect them to even regress backwards. You have to judge this regression. Is it fixable? Are they willing to fix it? Or, have they just replaced the behavior just long enough to get in your good graces?

As mentioned before, govern yourself accordingly. This will be a ongoing process. Replacing people is a separate process from replacing your behaviors. So, I recommend the mastering of replacing one's own behavior first.

You cannot control the actions of other people. You can control how their actions make you feel. Well, if you have a good grasp on your own behaviors and consciousness. You have to build up to maintaining relationships with people that offend you.

For people like me, it is natural to replace them. However, I am friends with some wonderful people. They know how to handle their offenders as gracefully as a friend. Others, like my granny, have a heart to forgive. Man, she has a super power.

I am a big enough to admit, replacing people has been a mistake sometimes. Some people are long gone, and they should be. Others I replaced out of immaturity and lack of experience. Life taught me quick. Especially in my professional life.

These people would come back around in some fashion. You find out years later they run with the group you want acceptance within. They probably did not have on their groups emblem while you were replacing them. Sometimes you do not realize the damage until you have missed the opportunity.

There is one more person I want to discuss. They will be a part of a group you desire. They will hold the access key to an opportunity you want desperately. However, they are not a good person.

They will use your need to rape your integrity. They will dangle that access key in front of you to get their needs met. Almost like making you dance on command. Be careful of them. They will appear inviting.

Once you get a sense of their motive, run for the hills. Their key is not worth your soul. There are predators that use their resources to trap others for their will. They have no regard for your personal well-being.

It is almost like dodging a pimp. This person is just getting something from their victim other than their body. Sometimes they get that too. You ever heard of "sleeping your way to the top"? As a woman, I will say it is real real.

There are other offenders that can do worse things. Revealing these things do not align with the point of this literature. The point is, you have to evaluate each offense. You have to evaluate the people person by person.

Failing to sift, cut back, and replace people in your life is dangerous. The people closest to you can be your biggest enemies. They put on as friends, the whole while they are a foe. The best imposters are never caught.

The people that you allow close to you have to watch. Their words have some importance. You want to watch their actions. Their words could be disguising their true intentions.

I am forgiving of many offenses. This is because I require a lot of forgiveness myself. I just have no tolerance for a snake. A snake is a person like the predator I mentions earlier.

A snake can also be someone who is jealous of you. They stick close to learn your moves. They wait for the right moment to strike you. Feeding them and showing the upmost loyalty will not protect you from their strike.

You cannot predict what every person will do. This is why it is imperative that you watch and take notes if you see something off. A little comment can be a sign of big jealousy. A brief move can reveal ill intentions.

I try to rebuild with others with lesser offenses. It is a learning experience for me and them. We both grow in some capacity if we can reconcile. Reconciliation is a friend of future opportunities.

Since you cannot predict the future, just cut people back. Replace them if you must. Just make sure you do not end up without a friend after all of your replacing. Make sure you are honest about your role in conflicts.

Working with people will be a waste if you cannot successfully replace your own behaviors. You will find yourself always justifying your bad behaviors. This justification is okay if you want to be alone. If you can master replacement behaviors in yourself, you will have more understanding for others.

Chapter 9: Mastering Replacement Behaviors

If you can master personal replacement behaviors, life should start turning around for you. If you have the replacement behaviors aligned to goals, you should see yourself coming closer to the goals. You should eventually see yourself take on new and positive rhythms. Some people will see results faster than others.

You may need to seek professional and licensed help if you try on your own with no results. Or if you try on your own and you are not happy with the results. A better life is obtainable for anyone willing to work for it. You may just need tools outside of this literature.

Learning to skillfully cut back instead of replacing people is its own doozy. It is worth the growth if you practice this. The rewards are distributed to you and the person you maintain the relationship with. Discernment is key in this category.

There is one last thing I want you to be mindful of. That thing is stagnancy. Mastering the skills I mentioned above can make one comfortable in life. After enough diligence, the rewards will make themselves pillows.

The hunger for more is appeased. The next thing you know, you are stagnant. I believe stagnancy is a choice. I have a point in life that I deem comfortable once I obtain it.

Mastering replacement behaviors creates a involuntary stagnancy in the beginning. The initial hunger that drove you to replace behaviors for a better cause will subside. It subsides with every goal obtained. It makes a person naturally comfortable. Comfortable people are susceptible to becoming stagnant.

It is great that you accomplish goals. I think it is important to celebrate each one along the way. This should be a bittersweet moment though. The accomplishing of one goal should signal the work beginning on another one.

You also have to be careful about accomplishing goals. People hope and pray for things fervently. They vow to give up almost anything for it. They know, and their God knows, they would not give up a dinner plate. Let alone anything else.

They pray for the thing a little more. When it arrives, something happens. They realize they do not want what they want. They either power through digging for something else or settle for what they have.

The strongest people have the energy to change their course. It is like working in a career for ten years and realizing you want to change. Some people will change. Most will remain in that career.

The change like other things require more process. New skills and education is necessary to change a career. This means new replacement behaviors have to be initiated as well. After spending years in one process, some people do not have the courage to start another one.

This change is not only true of a career. It is true of whatever you want it to be in life. The process of replacing behaviors can be applied to where ever you want it to go in life. Define your goal, initiate replacement behaviors, then manifest the goal through diligence.

You might have to apply it various times throughout your life. Matter of fact you should. You should be continuously attaining goals. This means you are constantly in a state of becoming better.

This is the opposite of stagnancy. Stagnancy can be stealthy itself. It will sneak in as a distraction. Once the distraction has you bound, the stagnancy sets in.

Keep in mind the distraction can be something that you like. This is the worst. You could be trapped in a rhythm of doing something that you like. If that thing is not profiting you or promoting growth, it is making you stagnant.

It is at this point the average are separated from the uber successful. I am speaking in terms of socioeconomics. The average are not bad people. Neither are the less than average.

The average and below make a conscious choice to slow down their progress. Sometimes life circumstances debilitate them. I know many that voluntarily settle. They get caught in life.

Their distractions hold more weight than their profits. They have a taste for more. They do not have a burning desire they are willing to act upon. They stay with their rhythm at a certain point instead of continuously replacing their behaviors.

The uber successful do the opposite. They do not stop. They keep going. They apply the work I suggest. They continuously replace behaviors.

They understand it is necessary for continuous elevation. They have a good grip on their rhythm, they can direct it as needed. Many times, this distraction is profitable goals. They have fun as well.

They just make sure the profitable behaviors take up more time than distractions. They understand stagnancy. They run far away from it. They do their best to stay progressive.

Anyone with sound mind and body can initiate replacement behaviors. I recommend defeating stagnancy for everyone. It sounds simple. However, it is heard to direct all of your behaviors towards your goals.

If you stay in the process, you will know when it is time to change. When you recalibrate periodically it will be evident. Sometimes you may even have to have an impromptu recalibration. New information can shake up your goals and change your direction.

Do not worry about the opinion of others, do what is best for you. No matter how old you get, you will have the same fears I mentioned earlier. It will just become easier to manage them as you get more disciplined. Never be afraid to change your mind or behavior.

The same people that will ostracize you, will not lend you a peanut butter and jelly sandwich. Yet, they will make their opinions clear as if they help with your monthly expenses. Do yourself a favor, think freely. You have to think in terms of your personal goals.

If you do make a decision to become stagnant, make sure it is a personal decision. Make sure you are financially stable without having to hustle later. There are people that become stagnant, again, because it feels good. Later in life they have to hustle to survive or depend on others.

Become stagnant at a good phase. For some that will be younger ages than others. It just depends on the effort applied. If you are watching someone. Make sure it is to take notes towards success. Some get caught up watching in envy.

Stagnancy is a two-sided dagger. It can hinder a person from achieving their goals. It can be a personal choice after adequate effort has been applied in an area. I suggest you stay away from the ones that stop your goals.

If you do dabble in a distraction, remember not to stay too long. It will become a part of your rhythm if you do. You want your rhythm to stay profitable. This will happen by sticking to profitable behaviors.

There is a lot in this book. Or I should say, checking yourself can be a lot. It is easy for us to check others. This book challenges you to check you so that you can be a better you.

Chapter 10: Making Replacement Behaviors Count

Mastering the process of replacing behaviors is difficult. In order to reach certain heights, it is necessary. Know where you are going and which behaviors to apply that are aligned. This type of discipline will unlock your greater self.

Replacement behaviors can give you the keys to a new life. For example, there are famous producers that were once homeless. Homeless was their status, but it was not their goal. If so, they would have stayed homeless.

Instead, they unlocked their greater selves. They replaced their behaviors until they came into the goals they had envisioned for themselves. If they had not replaced their behaviors, they would still be doing what homeless people do. They also had to have a unbreakable tenacity.

Imagine being homeless. It is hard right? Even if you have been there it is hard. You have to be strong to think, "despite where I am, I will be successful". They had to have unflinching will power to do things as if they were already there.

They would not allow the distraction of their circumstance to stop them. They powered through the continuous rejections that come with applying for a dream. They did what most people fail to do. They kept going no matter what.

Finding their greater self-brought about perks. The perks most people desire. The same people are not willing to put in the work for the perks, however.

The perk that attracts most attention is financial perks. Financial perks are a possibility when you unlock your greater self. It does not happen by miracle. An individual must market and sell themselves. They must offer a service or a product.

They also have the freedom to operate in secret. There are many talented people in the closet. They sing amazing at home where no one can hear. They write beautiful poetry that no one ever reads.

Another perk is associates. These associates are new people that you have to evaluate. Test them out, do not just give them your secrets.

Some are cunning enough to know they are being tested. Distribute thorough evaluations.

Everyone will want to be on board when you start being great. Some of these associates will be very lucrative. You will enter networks and groups of like successful people. More opportunities will also present themselves.

Always know the price you are paying. Not much comes free. Give the same opportunities that you wish to receive. You may have to give them to people who hold no immediate value. Look for potential when this happens.

Replacing behaviors and unlocking your greater self is a double-edged sword. As you elevate, you have to watch your attitude. You have to watch that elitist behaviors do not seep in. In simpler terms, remain humble.

The point of replacement behaviors should not to be used to exalt yourself over others. Check your motives. You should be working to make your generations financially stable. Your goals should include helping others the way you once needed help.

You have to be careful not to over indulge. When you have access to much, you are tempted by much. You have to be cautious not to deplete everything you earn as you go. Part of your goals should be residual resources. Involuntary circumstances can bring you down.

Summary:

As long as you are healthy, replace your behaviors to access the world you want to live in. It is ok to want more. Whoever tells you it is not, just does not believe in themselves. That is their problem, not yours.

Start by defining behavior and its role in your life. Behavior means different things to different individuals. You have to get a good grip on your own personal definition. This will help you know what you are replacing.

Then continue by identifying your own behaviors. Analyze their individual roles in your life. Toss out the ones that are hindering your progress in any area. You are essentially making room.

Make a conscious effort to break those unprofitable behaviors. It will take you some time. They are a part of your rhythm. You essentially have to reprogram yourself. Be patient.

Next define your goals. Again, you need to have a good idea of the direction you are going in. This will help you align and pick the behaviors conducive for you. Do not live a haphazard life. Always have a plan or a set of goals to follow.

If you have made it past the first stages, you might be on to something. Take a in-depth look at your goals. Research what behaviors are necessary to achieve them. A good way to do this is by finding someone who is already there. If you have access to the person great.

If not, access a biography. It would be good to know the challenges that come with your journey. You can also save some time by paying attention to how they defeated that challenge. Do not waste time reinventing the wheel.

Activate these replacement behaviors in your life with a purpose. Be ready for fatigue during the process. Prepare to run into circumstances that will threaten your progress. Just keep going and you will get there.

Remember to recalibrate when necessary. This time is needed to sift through wasteful behaviors and propensities. It is a review of your goals. Maybe even a realignment.
I recommended doing this in a schedule. You might need to do it on a whim. This is ok. The schedule just ensures it happens. This is an effort to prevent stagnancy.

Be mindful of new distractions as you replace behaviors. They will attack various areas of your life. A distraction is not always an attack either. Sometimes it is a voluntary indulgence.

Have discernment when this happens. Watch for distractions that can be turned into to opportunities. Be sure to avoid the distractions that are a barrier to your goals. If you fall backwards be sure to get up quick.

Make sure you do not replace people as rapidly as you do behaviors. You have to work relationships with people. Even when they offend you, you have to work on reconciling. It is safer for your long term. It also makes you a better person in return.

Be willing to be dynamic. After your hunger to be great is fed, do not forget to keep elevating. Sometimes being comfortable can lead to being stagnant. Only do this when you are financially safe.

When you bring it all together; greatness can happen. The greatness will be determined by the individual. All individuals measure greatness by different scales. Your goals are your personal scales.

If you fail to use replacement behaviors, life can be hard. Many elevations that I know of require some type of behavior change. I think the media fools people into thinking they can make it without changes. It is possible, just almost impossible.

As you make attempts to access a better life, you will have to meet requirements. The consequences of not meeting these requirements can be stagnancy. Stagnancy should only be ok if you are financially free.

That is why I am still working myself.

Be ready to put in some work. You may have to revisit some steps but keep going. You only have your best life to gain. No one can do it for you. They are busy working on their own goals.

Most people think that trying one time and failing is enough. Since most new things are not a natural part of your rhythm, I can almost guarantee you will experience failure. Just learn from it. Then keep going. It is only really failure if you quit.

A Note About Mental Distractions

(Excerpt from Deceit of Distractions)

Mental distractions in my opinion are the most detrimental of them all. Mental distractions can be invisible to the naked eye. They are not tangible like mistresses and overspent money. Still the presence of mental distractions can be just as eroding.

One can identifying a relationally distracted man by his infidelity. It is easy to spot a financially distracted woman when her finances are pledged to frivolous spending habits. The spiritually distracted are marked by their lack of moral compass and respect of values. Mental distractions take a bit more digging to expose.

Some mental distractions are as harmless as sulking over a failed exam. Things happen daily that cause us to give negative energy attention. We are human. The dangerous part of giving negative energy attention is the possibility of not moving past it by a reasonable time.

Negativity only begets negativity. Sometimes we become distracted by so many small negative things, life seems like a big negative blur. You have to proactively throw off negative distraction with positive affirmations. This is easier said than done.

Let's look at the exam example. If I make a failing grade in my first class and negate to throw it off, it will amplify the negativity of the next negative occurrence. If I fail to throw off the next few negative distractions, the negativity starts to snowball. By the end of the day, I will think I had a terrible day.

The reality is, my day is not terrible, I am just letting mental distractions blind me to positive aspects of my day. The negativity also prevents me from making rational decisions about how to improve my day. Negative thoughts are like cancer. They eat away at positivity and consume your mental space with their negativity.

I like to call mental distractions phantoms. We fight them and their potential harm daily. We rarely stop to acknowledge that half of the things we were distracted by in the past never came to fruition. This truth alone should prevent one from indulging in negative mental distractions.

These phantoms haunt our goals and future dreams. They remind us of our inconsistencies and lack of resources. They prevent us from taking vital and initial steps to success. They stand in the way of those that yield to them and steal their potential for success.

These phantoms invade our present too. They constantly remind us of losing our current status. This can be at work, home, or various area in life. The try to entice us to give up. These phantoms are not age biased.

They lie to us that others are against us. Sadly, those same people do not have us in mind. They are too busy fighting their own phantoms. Keep this in mind when someone gives you a "vibe" when you read their facial expression. Yes, they possess a vibe, just maybe not concerning you.

Everyday stressors give life to the mental distractions or phantoms. Most of us interact with other through your day. Some do have the luxury of staying isolated in their home three hundred and sixty-five days of the week,

I think. People bring uncontrollable variables that me respectfully tolerate.

Human error brings unforeseen circumstances. Sometimes these errors are not committed by us, but they still affect us. Everyday a new challenge presents itself as a new mental distraction depending on your agenda. I work in behavior, I wrestle with negativity for a living.

Other phantoms purposely come from your past to mentally distract you. They remind you of past sins and shortcomings. They threaten you with exposing new associates to old skeletons. They will isolate you with fear of what happened to stunt what will be.

Mental distractions from your past play on failed attempts as well. When the greatest philosophers and successful people in the world are asked the key to success, they almost all agree on failure. They use failure as a strategy to extrapolate learning opportunities. The meet failure with open arms knowing failure is a component of success.

If you are average, failure can have a devastating effect on you. I think people forget everyone fails. Instead of letting it go, a mentally distracted person will facilitate negative thoughts about failure. They will use failure as an excuse to not try again.

The whole while, no one is aware you are fighting a single thing. This is what makes mental distractions so dangerous. Loved ones can intervene where they see need. Everyone is not strong enough to cry for help. Some are too ashamed to.

I have found that people that are highly and mentally distracted live very haphazard lives. As a disclaimer, I am not living to my fullest potential. I am still working to reach my personal goals and pinnacles. However, you can tell I am going somewhere.

I can tell when others are going somewhere as well. We all are susceptible to mental distractions. The ones that yield to the negative and unprofitable ones the most are obvious too. I am so sure because I used to struggle with some of the same distractions.

Self-discipline must be master or almost master to beat mental distractions. The discipline will teach you to set goals. It will give you the tools to meet the goal. Earl Nightingale said that most people cannot reach goals because it becomes boring.

Mental distractions might be the most deceitful of all distractions. Beside the phantoms, a person has to control the illusion of their perception. When a person is highly enraged, their perception of most things will be negative. If a person is experiencing unflinching peace, they can extrapolate positivity from the worse scenario.

Even though I struggle with anger, I believe it is safer to choose peace on purpose. Peace softens the spirit and clears the mind. I think the spirit is the gateway to the mentality. Our mentality is the reaction to what our spirits receive continuously.

Therefore, if you constantly receive peace, you tend to be a peaceful person. The angered let negative energy manifest inside until it is excreted from their actions. When we let mental distractions and negative energy in, we run the risk of infecting our mental state.

Medical books call this phenomenon mental illness.

I am not a doctor. Nothing in this book should be taken as medical advice. There are people with mental illnesses caused by heredity and medical factors. There is also a population of people who suffer from self-inflicted mental illness.

I have seen two things be true in my life. One, a man was given a two week notice to live. At the time, he worked three jobs. He went to work seven days a week. This was two years ago.

He is in his 70's and alive and well. He picks his grandkids up from school. He was forced to retire, but he is still enjoying life. He has physical restrictions, but he prefers that over time restrictions on his life.

Two, another person in my life is constantly ill. She watches all types of shows that expose her to various diseases. She is constantly looking up every hurt and tingle to diagnose herself. When she hears of a new prognosis she aligns herself to fit the criteria.

The first person was focused on healing. Let's be clear, yes it takes more than focus. You cannot smoke, drink, and eat junk food for 60 years and expect a miracle. Still, part of healing is focus.

The second person is still to this day complaining of some ailment. That time she is taking to be distracted by phantoms of sickness could be used to manifest profits. She has had this habit for so many years, at this point it is a negative hypnotic rhythm. I believe this is a scary mental distraction to have.

One person is mentally focused. He refused to allow a trained medical professional steer his destiny. He had the power to think for himself. He could have chosen to accept the death sentence.

The other person is not dead. But how alive are you when you are constantly distracted by something not happening? The more she allows herself to mentally distracted, the more time she triggers her body to manifest the sickness. You see the folly in mental distractions yet?

143

I grew up believing that if you heard voices in your head you were crazy. I do not believe anyone specifically told me that. I gathered that information from seeing tv and people with "voices in their head". It was assumed knowledge.

The struggle was I heard voices in my head. I used to try and suppress it with music or directed thoughts. As I grew up, I realized those voices were not voices. It was my mentality.

I just attributed it to voices because it is how I naturally receive information, through sound. The mentality is the thing that reminds me to remind myself. The mentality is an accumulation of all images and sounds I have been exposed to. It gives me encouragement or discouragement depending on my choice.

The mentality is not biased. It is not a tyrant. It allows us to indulge in the energy of our choosing. If we allow mental distractions in, it receives them with open arms. If we decide to ignore mental distractions, it rolls with that decision to.

A person has to be a steward over their mentality. Mental distractions can come wrapped in pretty bows. Mental distractions will present themselves in the form of a handsome man. Mental distractions can be something you in fact enjoy.

I suffer from mental distractions. I do not know who does not. The important thing is managing those distractions. This is where goals play another role.

If you formulate goals and timelines, you are less likely to be mentally distracted. If you lack self-discipline this will not work. The goals serve as a time filler. Goals just happen to also have the benefit of building futures too. Positive goals that is.

Mental distractions do not always have an evil agenda. Sometimes we have to mentally distract ourselves to save ourselves. I get it. I just advise one never to stay mentally distracted too long.
Always recalibrate and being yourself back to reality. Being mentally distracted on purpose is a sign you are running from something. At some point you have to stop running and start winning. Winning is found in finishing.

Mental distractions hinder a person from finishing. They induce stagnancy and failure. They may even feel good. The reality is there is a reality. Be focused is the only way to positively change any reality.

Thank you for reading.
-Toy Taylor

About the
Author

Toy Taylor is a native of Waco, Tx. She currently manages a behavior unit in Austin, Tx. For more information and other works by the author please visit toytaylorbooks.com.

Other Books:

A Peace of Edith

Toy Taylor

Publish 5 Books in 5 Months or Less

I have many other books!
Check out my site: toytaylorbooks.com

Made in the USA
Columbia, SC
14 November 2023

26309659R00093